T0142526

A Cup of Coffee
and
A Good Book

Dr. Glenn A. Mills

authorHOUSE®

AuthorHouse™
1663 Liberty Drive
Bloomington, IN 47403
www.authorhouse.com
Phone: 1-800-839-8640

Published by AuthorHouse 11/17/2014

ISBN: 978-1-4969-2808-5 (sc)
ISBN: 978-1-4969-2807-8 (e)

Table of Contents

Cherish The Moments

· ·

It's the beauty of an early morning sunrise,
    It's the smell of daffodils in the spring.
It's the splendor of the last moments of sunset,
    It's the awe when you hear a robin sing.

Special moments just show up,
    Just hoping to be found,
Bringing forth a gentle smile,
    To replace that unpleasant frown.

It's a baby's first steps,
    It's their first words said.
One day you hand them the keys.
    It's that awful feeling of dread.

It's that time at the beach,
    When your toes met the sand.
It's that first real date,
    When they reached for your hand.

It's that moment of praise,
    For something done right.
It's those moments of victory,
    It was the really scary night.

It was the kiss, and the hug,
    It was magic, it was love.
As for your heart,
    It touched every part.

You stood by their bed,
    It was the things they said.
How could you not cry?
    It was time for goodbye.

The list could go on,
    Of the things to remember,
Each year will offer more,
    From January to December.

So remember these moments,
    Never allow them to perish.
They form who we really are,
    These are the moments we cherish.

Priceless

· · · · · · · · · · ·

It's more valuable, more precious than gold.
It's greater than all the wealth, your pockets could hold.

It will give you something the world cannot give.
It can remain with you, so long as you live.

It will help you sleep, and bring gentle rest.
Once you have it, you can pass every test.

It calms your spirit, and it comforts your soul.
Though time may pass, it never grows old.

It stops the panic, brings things under control.
It's unmoved by the lies, that are so often told.

It adds years to your life, and much joy too.
Helps start every day, feeling fresh and anew.

So what is this thing that we all hope to find?
It comes from God, it's Peace of Mind.

Friends

· · · · · · · · · · ·

They stand by you, through thick and thin.
They hold you up, till the very end.

They laugh with you, and they cry.
They know your pain, they hear your sigh.

They remind you often, don't ever give in.
Keep on smiling, and up with the chin.

A pat on the back, they joyfully give.
Without them it seems we could not live.

They tell us the truth, may not feel good.
They encourage us to act, the way that we should.

No matter the distance, no matter the need.
They will be there, with the quickest of speed.

They remain true, while others pretend.
Who are they you may ask? We call them, Friend.

That Ol' Barn

· · · · · · · · · · · · · · · · · ·

Have you ever wondered in some odd way,
If old buildings could talk, what would they say?
They would truly have us under their spell,
As we listened to the stories they could tell.

Stories of people who entered their doors,
And all the activities that crossed their floors.
Who looked in their windows and who looked out,
Much could be told, and to that there's no doubt.

How about the storms that they went through,
And the peaceful early mornings all covered in dew.
They could tell of times some good and some bad,
Of the people around them who were happy or sad.

They could tell of the work done there and the times of rest,
And of those who built them and who loved them best.
They are not just old buildings or a wooden shell,
They are lingering memories with a story to tell.

Dr. Glenn A. Mills

The Beach

· · · · · · · · · · · · ·

It's the sun in your face,
It's the laid back pace.
It's the sound of the waves,
It's these moments you crave.

The wind is steadily blowing,
As your excitement is showing.
You walk in the sand,
Or you lay out and tan.

The pelicans are soaring
The seagulls are exploring.
Seashells are free for the taking,
Its memories you are making.

It's the pictures you take,
If but for the moments sake.
It's the place that you love,
It's your gift from above.

There are few things as neat,
As a peaceful day at the Beach.

Special Days

· · · · · · · · · · · · · · · ·

In the moment when I gave up
Had no reason to press on.
God sent you to comfort me
And give my heart a song.

Like the Rainbow after the rain,
Like the healing after the pain.
You touched me in such a way,
That I can never be the same.

You helped drive away my fears,
And the hurts of all the years.
You made me feel alive again,
You brushed away my tears.

My heart was like a winter,
It was dreary and it was cold.
But you were like springtime,
When the flowers would unfold.

My world became alive again,
Everything again was new.
It was all because God loves me,
And He knew I needed you.

But like the seasons, they all transition,
So has the time of your special mission.
And yet it's never easy to let go,
Of the things that helped you grow.

Part of me will go with you,
As we go in different ways.
I thank you for the memories.
And ALL the special days.

Let It Go

. . . .

How could you know
At the very start,
It would fill your mind
It would touch your heart.
It became a part of you
It innocently took hold.
It moved you in ways
That are yet to be told.
It gave you much joy,
When things were grim.
Brought light to your soul
When your world was dim.
It met a deep need
If but for a season.
It made no demands
It sought no reason.
But now you sense
It's slipping away.
And with all your heart
You can't make it stay.
So appreciate the times
It touched you so.
And ask God for strength
To now let it go.

The Puppy In Blue

Just look at that face,
Those fluffy ears too.
The one in the picture,
The puppy in blue.

Cute as a button,
He is looking at you.
Yes the one in the sweater,
The puppy in blue.

He is cuddly and soft,
His hair trimmed anew.
That handsome young mutt,
The puppy in blue.

To get your attention,
He will nibble and chew.
But who could get mad,
At the puppy in blue.

He might rip up the paper,
Eat holes in your shoe.
He will steal your heart,
That puppy in blue.

So give him some love,
And he will love you.
He will always be faithful,
Your puppy in blue.

Dr. Glenn A. Mills

The Fat Monster

. . . .

I stepped on the scales,
Just the other day.
Much to my surprise,
Much to my dismay.

This can't be right,
Something must be wrong.
It was just a few days ago,
It has not been that long.

My weight was perfect,
Was just what I wanted.
But now I've been stalked.
And I have been haunted.

To my mind comes a name,
For which I can blame.
This excess that I have,
This fat I have gained.

It's the FAT Monster,
That relentless beast.
Shows up at every meal,
He loves every feast.

He attacked from nowhere,
When I was not looking.
He hides in the desserts,
He loves country cooking.

In most foods I crave,
What is it I now see?
It's that FAT Monster,
And He's laughing at me.

So I've made up my mind,
And I said to myself.
If I change my diet,
I will starve him to death.

And how will I know,
He does slowly die?
Keep checking the scales,
Because they do not lie.

Dr. Glenn A. Mills

The Victory Run

· · · · · · · · · · · · · · · · · · ·

The weather was perfect,
And the mood was right.
So I decided to go run,
While there was still light.

So I put on my sweats,
And my running shoes too.
And off for my run,
With the highway in view.

Which way should I go?
To the left or the right.
Either way I looked,
The road went out of sight.

But in an instant I saw,
A flashback from the past.
When I was much younger,
I could run so fast.

I was quick like the wind,
Built for the speed.
Fast as the tiger,
Enduring like the steed.

So off I'm now running,
With this image in my head.
Traveling at a pace,
That could soon find me dead.

Not far down the road,
My heart was a race.
But I have set my sights,
And I have set my pace.

Now my lungs are burning,
My face is red too.
My legs are soon tiring,
And I'm coming unglued.

Reality quickly sets in,
I came to my senses.
Overtaken by exhaustion,
It broke down my defenses.

So I said to myself,
Rome wasn't built in a day.
Plus no one wants to die,
From running this way.

But still I made progress,
And I covered much land.
Was the longest half mile,
I believe I ever ran.

Dr. Glenn A. Mills

What Was He Thinking

Why would He give up,
His great throne above.
To come to this planet,
It had to be love.

But came He did,
Laid in a manger with hay.
What a glorious event,
What a magnificent day.

So there began the journey,
His walk back toward home.
Much work was to be done,
Before returning to His Throne.

He lived and He laughed,
He cried and He loved.
He even showed us,
His Father above.

He taught us the Word,
He touched and He healed.
And the plan of salvation,
He did so plainly reveal.

But what stirs me the most,
With the passing of time.
When He hung on the Cross,
What was on His mind?

Forever I was changed,
When finally I did see.
When He died on that Cross,
He was thinking of Me.

He Will Meet You There

As I awake another Sunday,
Thanking God it's not Monday.
Among the first things I say,
"Thank You, LORD, for another day."

But today is more special,
Than the six yet to be.
It is a special day of worship,
To the God who created me.

So I will get myself ready,
And I will put on my best.
And start praising His name,
For how I have been blessed.

With the strength He provides,
It's off to church I will go;
To meet with all the others,
Who also love Him so.

I will gladly give Him praise,
Which He is worthy of;
For all He has done for me,
And His overflowing love.

My tithe I gladly give Him,
Which He freely gave to me.
For I would have nothing,
But for His great generosity.

I will lift my hands to Him,
I will sing of His great love.
I will worship and adore Him,
As He watches from above.

But why go to Church when,
You can worship anywhere?
It's because of His promise,
That He would meet me there.

What Are You Trusting In

Big houses can make us,
   The talk of the town.
Sadly my dear friend,
   Houses can burn down.

And cars when new,
   They sparkle and shine.
But they can also fade,
   With the passing of time.

The clothes we thought,
   Would make us so glad.
Like many things we bought,
   Were just a passing fad.

And the money we say,
   If we just had enough.
Then we could go out,
   And purchase more stuff.

But all the material things,
   Will soon be gone and past,
Only what is done for Jesus,
   Will be the things that last.

God's Precious Love

It took away my sin,
It removed my shame.
It gave me a new life,
It gave me a new name.

Brought me out of the dark,
Into His glorious light.
It gave me a fresh start,
And a reason to do right.

It chased away my doubts,
And calmed all of my fears.
It filled my heart with love,
Wiped away all my tears.

Gave me peace for today,
Expectancy for my tomorrow.
Brought joy into my life,
It removed all my sorrow.

It has given me reason,
A desire in which to live,
An everlasting love,
A heart wanting to give.

It's as sweet as the morning,
As the song of the dove.
It has changed me forever,
God's Most Precious Love.

Thy Will
· · · · · · · · · · ·

From the early dawn, till the setting sun,
Not my will LORD, but Thine be done.
May I walk the way, LORD, You would walk.
May I talk the way, LORD, You would talk.

I pray this flesh of mine, would surely die.
So your total desire, LORD, I would satisfy.
May each decision and choice I make,
Be deeply decided for your name's sake.

May my hand not touch the unclean things,
But hold tightly the blessings obedience brings.
May the thoughts I think be holy and true,
May my mind be fully consumed with You.

May my lips speak only comfort and peace,
May my soul in You find sweet release.
May my eyes be guarded from lingering sin,
But look with compassion for the souls of men.

May my ears, LORD, be sensitive to hear,
Your abiding steps that are always near.
May my heart with love daily grow stronger,
May my time in Your presence grow longer.

I pray I am stirred and broken until,
My only desire LORD is to do THY WILL.

Help Me Lord

. . . .

Lord, I want to be like You,
In all the things I do and say.
Not just for this moment,
But for each and every day.

I want to deeply love others,
With a love that's real and true.
I want to treat them fairly,
Regardless of the things they do.

May I never assume anything,
But give others loving respect.
May thoughts of their perfection,
Be something I never expect.

Lord, may my fleshly opinions,
Never once be given voice.
But let my mouth be full of praise,
And let my heart always rejoice.

I want to treat all others, Lord,
The way You have treated me.
Then my flesh will lose control,
And I will be gloriously free.

God's Desire

· · · · · · · · · · · · · · · ·

He is Ever-present, He is Majesty.
He is Ever-lasting, He is Eternity.

But of all the places, our eyes may see,
Where is the place God longs to be?

Surely the mountains, so high and grand,
Maybe the Beach, with miles of sand?

Maybe the ocean, with waters so deep;
Could be the canyons, with walls so steep.

Might be the skies, that hover above,
Or the arms of a Mother, giving her love.

How about the desert, a very quiet place,
Somewhere to rest, and slow down the pace.

Maybe the rainforest, or the jungles so green,
Might be a river, a lake, a pond, a stream.

How about the mansion, a house on a hill,
Could be a cabin, or a beautiful old mill.

But of all the places, that God could be,
He desires the heart of You and Me.

Listen

· · · · · · · · ·

If you listen intently, you can hear,
The sound of something most precious and dear.

It gave justice to the abused and oppressed,
It broke the power that had many distressed.

It gave hope and comfort to those it would touch,
But who could have imagined it would cost so much.

It traveled abroad to places both near and far.
Could be found in the trenches, the dirt and mar.

It heeded the call and it met the enormous need.
It responded to the hurts, the afflictions and pleas.

It gave itself completely both day and night.
It represents what is truly honorable and right.

It endured through conditions far from nice.
It would willingly give the ultimate sacrifice.

'Tis freedom you hear coming up from the ground.
Wherever the blood of an American Soldier is found.

Ever Present

· · · · · · · · · · · · · · · · ·

Before I ever knew about You,
You were already loving me.
While I was still a captive,
You had Grace to set me free.

When I felt alone and scared,
Your peace came gently through.
Even when I didn't understand,
Even before I knew it was You.

When my valley was too deep,
And my mountain was too high.
You were always guarding over me,
From Your throne above the sky.

You sent things to bless me,
And things to help me grow.
In more ways than I can count,
Your love would always show.

No matter what I faced,
No matter how big the test.
You always knew what I needed,
You always knew what was best.

I can look back with joy,
And see Your loving care.
I know with all confidence,
That You were always there.

So as I continue on my journey,
Till I reach my heavenly home.
Because You, God, are ever-present,
I know I will never be alone.

Cross Over

· · · · · · · · · · · · ·

Let me cross over
At the boundary I stand,
To life that's eternal
In that promised land.

Let me cross over
Your face to see,
For worldly sin you died,
That I could go free.

Let me cross over
To suffer no more,
As I stand near Jordan
That far distant shore.

Let me cross over
My troubles are past
To my home eternal
I have reached it at last.

Let me cross over
To leave fear behind,
To step into Heaven
With newness of mind.

Let me cross over
To embrace thy Son,
Who gave me the victory
My battle's been won.

As I cross over
That boundary of time,
A clear path I leave
For those left behind.

The path that I followed
Was neither stone nor mud,
For Jesus is the road,
It is paved with His blood.

Will you cross over
At the journey's end?
Are you on the path
Where true life begins?

Have you taken the Savior
Whose blood met the cost?
Or will you stand at eternity
Without him, and lost?

Weep Not For Me

Here lies my body for all to see,
Lift up your head, weep not for me.

I lived my life so full and so free,
I thank the Father, weep not for me.

To be with Jesus for eternity,
And my dreams fulfilled, weep not for me.

I treated others so humbly,
As I had wished to be treated, weep not for me.

I waited on the Lord, oh so patiently,
It was worth it all, weep not for me.

I strived to be for God all I could be,
To Him I was someone, weep not for me.

I did my time and I said my plea,
I enjoyed my life, weep not for me.

Though I leave you now with my memory,
I am now with Jesus, so rejoice for me!

Church On The Hill

· ·

In Virginia, just outside Wytheville,
You are sure to get a spiritual thrill.
If you will stop by and visit,
The little church there on the hill.

It has white siding and the top is green,
It's the most precious church you've ever seen.
It can't help but to make your day,
When you see all the places, there to pray.

Inside it's so beautiful and so exciting,
It's very comforting and spiritually inviting.
The little pews give visitors a place to rest,
And the atmosphere will leave you blessed.

There is a sweet presence that abides,
You know it's Jesus standing by your side.
It's open to all both day and night,
A place where you can get your heart right.

I'm so glad I found that place there in time,
That calmed my heart and touched my mind.
Never will I forget that it was God's Will,
That I find that church on the side of the hill.

Walking With Jesus

He calmed the waves
He calmed the sea,
He gave His life
For you and me.

Though troubles come
As years may go,
His arms are open
His love to show.

When peace we need
His face we seek,
He gives peace freely
It's ours to keep.

In life's storms
Of doubt and fear,
Just call His name
He will draw near.

He's always there
When burdens start,
To calm the mind
To soothe the heart.

He knows the joy
When a child is born,
He knows the sorrow
Of those who mourn.

He walks beside us
From day to day,
He stops and listens
When we pray.

His hand in ours
We are never alone,
He leads us toward heaven
Our eternal home.

He can be trusted
In loss or in gain,
In our moment of laughter
Or our moment of pain.

So put in His hands
Your life and your will,
He will calm your troubles
Saying, "Peace Be Still."

Ever Met The 'Happens'?

Those who remember what happened.
Those who wait for things to happen.
Those who watch things happen.
Those who wonder what happened.
Those who discuss what might happen.
Those who say it can't happen.
Those who wish things would happen.
But thank God for those who MAKE things happen.

Time Spent

Time spent with God is priceless.
Time spent at work is financially beneficial.
Time spent with loved ones is emotionally fulfilling.
Time spent relaxing is physically refreshing.
Time spent in a classroom is educational.
Time spent in the Bible is spiritually enlightening.
Time spent in prayer is empowering.
Time spent with the wrong people is dangerous.
Time spent on hobbies can be costly.
However, time spent doing nothing is a waste.

True Faith is:

On your mind,
In your heart,
Across your lips,
Against your enemy,
Over your situation,
And out of your hands.

Soar

You can never soar above your situation, circumstances or crisis until you first spread your wings of faith and ride the wind of God's presence and allow Him to carry you where He desires.

Destined

Divine
Energy
Spiritually
Teaching
Individuals
New
Enlightment
Daily

In Jesus We Are: Perfect

Perfected
Empowered
Righteous
Fearless
Excited
Complete
Thankful

Tears

Tangible
Emotions
Affirming
Reality
Sincerely

Bible:

Blessed Information Bestowing Life Eternal

Your Choice

To complain about your circumstance is Self-pity.
To accept your current circumstance as beyond chance is Complacency.
To take responsibility for your circumstance is Reality.
Trusting God to grow you through your current circumstance is Destiny.

Comparison

It is somewhat strange that the very thing that is supposed to liberate us has often made prisoners of us. Just my thoughts on the cell phone. What if the Bible meant as much to us as our cell phones? Someone would be quick to say, *"But I have the Bible in my phone."* While that may be true the question then would be, *"Do you use it?"*

Prepared

Never ask God to take you to something unless you are willing to go through something to get there. The something God may require you to go through will make you stronger and wiser in preparation for the place or position you want to go to. Falling down is easy, but climbing upward requires determination and endurance.

I Can

Regardless of my situation or circumstance, it is well with my soul. I am leaning on those everlasting arms of my Daddy, God, who cares for me. I have nothing to fear because my hope is in the LORD, from whence my strength comes. He is the Lifter of my head and the Protector of my mind. I CAN do ALL things though Christ who strengthens me.
Can I get a Witness!

Stand Strong

We are never defeated unless we believe we are defeated. God made us more than conquerors in Christ Jesus. We can say life is not fair and feel sorry for ourselves, or we can hold our heads up by the power of God in us and walk in victory. It is time we put Satan where he belongs; under our feet!

Content

While I do not have what I often think I want, I truly have at this moment, everything I need. I am quickly learning that less is more. It is in our times of decrease that God brings increase. May I soon become so small in myself and Jesus becomes so large in me, that I am not seen at all, but Him only in all I say and do.

Rejoice

Sometimes it would be so easy to complain about having a hard day until you suddenly remember you were blessed of God to even have another day at all. Press on with Praise!

Example

Because we do not always know all the reasons people do things that is all the more reason to pray for them instead of casting our opinions so quickly. God knows the situation much better than we do. How often have we had others say hurtful things about us when they had no idea what was happening to us at the time. If nothing else we can set a good example for others to follow.

Sunday

Sunday is the first day of the week, not the last. The way we start anything, will often determine how we finish. Is there any better way to start our week or day than with God? I think not! Our greatest blessings are found when we put God first in all things. Go to God's House on Sunday with expectancy. Worship Him! Praise Him! Honor Him! Seek His direction. Talk with Him and listen for His reply. This is the day the Lord has made, let US rejoice and be glad in it.

Real Friends

God, thank you so much for real friends. Those who love me no matter what. They encourage me when I need it most. They never judge me or doubt me. They see past my flaws and see the good in me. They pray with me and for me. They wish me only the best. I could never say enough about the real friends. They are handpicked by you Lord, thank you.

Assurance

I am going to have a really awesome day, where everything works out to my good. I am going to have peace and joy. I am going to enjoy every moment and learn from today's many activities. How can I be sure that such a day is possible? I am going to let God lead the way, guard my lips and guide my steps.

Loneliness

Loneliness does not stem from a body not touched but a heart not filled. Jesus said He would never leave us nor would He forsake us. Let Him fill your heart.

Weather

Sometimes the Lord wants us all to Himself so He may allow something like weather to confine us. Then, He waits on us to seek Him out. In these moments we have plenty of time to pray to Him, study His Word and meditate on His goodness. Sing praises to His name and worship Him. Don't miss such a blessed opportunity to know Him better.

Remember 9-11

On this day may we be reminded how quickly our freedoms can be attacked and serious damage can be done. But if it must be, then let us arise from our complacent state and fight to regain the freedoms we may have taken for granted and thank the enemy for awakening the sleeping giant within us.

Live Loud

As long as there is breath in your body there is opportunity to reach higher, go further, laugh louder, love deeper, try harder, think greater, be more, and seize the moments of life while we still have them. Don't waste another moment on what could have been, should have been or might have been. Live for today as if it were your last day to be able to live unrestricted.

Comfort

Any joy, peace or comfort we find outside of God's approval will be temporary, limited and short lived. All we need, is in who God is. He knows what we need, when we need it and how we need it. Trust Him today! Cast you cares upon the Lord for He cares for you.

Risen

Jesus is risen! He not only died for our sins but also defeated death, hell and the grave on our behalf. He rose from the dead, therefore granting us new life and eternal life. Today we can celebrate our King of kings and Lord of lords. Our sins are paid in full and our eternity is secure in Jesus Christ. Thank you Lord!

Old School

Many of the values we label as "Old School" are in reality Biblical Principles that were upheld by the generation we grew up with. Sadly, too many of today's generation are Biblically illiterate, therefore they have little, to no, knowledge of what is truth.

Faith

If you have it all figured out in life, then chances are it is not faith. True faith is often doing what we have no idea how to do, going in a direction of which you don't know the destination, and believing everything will work out just because God said it would.

God Is

Your first step to greatness is in trusting our great God.
Your shortest route to wisdom is to be led by our all-knowing God.
Your way to true strength is to be empowered by our all-mighty God.
Your best way to know love is to be consumed by our God who is Love.

Even When

Lord, even when I feel I have let you down, You lift me up.
Even when I don't talk to you, softly, You speak to me.
Even when I'm not searching for You, lovingly, You watch over me.
Even when it seems I give so little, You give completely.
Even when I'm slow doing Your Will, patiently You wait.
Even when I don't know what to do, You have a perfect plan for me.

Evaluation

Before we tell God what we will do for Him, we would do well to evaluate what we are currently doing. If we are not faithful with little, how can He trust us with much?

Choice

I would rather live with two regrets than with one moment of complacency. At least I attempted something! My life's biggest regret would be that I did nothing.

Declaration

Our enemy is only as big as we allow him to be. If we know Christ and He is Lord of our lives, then we have within us everything we need to walk in victory and power. Greater is He (Jesus) that is in me than he (Satan) that is in the world. Live in the light of truth in Christ and you will never be overtaken by the lies of darkness. This is the day our Lord hath made, let us rejoice and be glad in it.

Promotion

What many would call a "Wilderness" is really a place of learning and new opportunity. It is a place where our pride is defeated and a new found humility makes us usable again. It is a place where we can receive our new assignment for greater dreams than the ones we thought we had lost.

Our Current Situations Are:

Walls that can stop us,
Blocks that can trip us,
Lessons that can teach us,
Steps that can promote us,
Tools that can build us.
It's our choice!

Walk It Out

· · · · · · · · · · · · · ·

Disappointments are like grapes, they seem to come in bunches. And, sadly, they will come when we least expect them.

So what can we do when faced with another disappointment? Well, if disappointments come like grapes, then treat them like grapes. Press them until you have squeezed every bit of good you can get out of them.

In olden days, and in some places today, people would put the ripe grapes in an open type barrel and they would walk on the grapes with their bare feet so they actually felt the grapes being pressed. God gives us authority through Christ to put a lot of things under our feet.

So what good can come from a disappointment one might ask? Much! Disappointments can teach us lessons about life.
They can challenge us to try harder, go further and reach higher. They can get us out of our comfort zones and into new opportunities. Or they can defeat us. It's up to us.

So anyone dealing with some type of disappointment? Put it in the barrel of God's presence. Prepare yourself with prayer and thanksgiving.

Now jump on in and walk that disappointment out until the wine of great blessings and new opportunity flow.

Circumstances

Life can sometimes be very disappointing and heart breaking. There are so many things out of our control. One day you stand facing the sun as it warms your face and heart. The next day you are in a hurricane, holding on for dear life. One moment there is the sound of laughter and the next the tears of sorrow.

No one is exempt from experiencing those unpredictable, unexplainable moments in life. It's not that you did anything wrong. Things just happen. Life happens.

But our only constant is that JESUS said He would never leave us nor ever forsake us. No matter what we face He is closer than a brother. He will rejoice with us on the good days and hold our hand and lead us through the tough days.

God Knows Best

· · · · · · · · · · · · · · · · · · ·

This ain't Burger King!!!! This is, God is King! Allow me to explain. I was reminded by a really dear friend today that God always knows what is best. At BK you go in and place your order. You tell them exactly what you want and how you want it and if you are so bold, also, when you want it. And in a fairly short time, there it is. Doesn't matter that you might be overweight, have high blood pressure or some other health issue; they give you what you want. Why? Because all they want is your money.

But with God it's very different indeed. You can place your spiritual double whopper with large fries order if you want too, but don't be surprised if you find a spiritual salad with water sitting on your blessing tray. But, *"That's not what I ordered,"* we might say. And, our loving God and Father would smile and say, *"That is right, but this is what is BEST for you right now."* Why? Because He loves us and KNOWS what is best for us ALL the time. It is for that reason when we pray, God may not answer the way we want but will answer in a way that is best.

Let's face the facts, we often pray selfishly. Most times we have an idea of how we think God should answer. The problem with that, is we can't see into the future or even comprehend how getting OUR way will affect someone else.

But God knows ALL and He will do what is best. So with that, the best thing we can do is pray as best we know how and TRUST DADDY to do what is best. And who knows, if we eat enough salads, He may just one day allow us to have that Double Whopper with large fries blessing.

Integrity

· · · · · · · · · · · ·

The Word tells us that whether we eat or drink, or what so ever we do, do ALL to the glory of God. I would say that covers everything in our lives.

Of the many things that seem to be slipping from our generation, Integrity is at the top of the list. Integrity is doing the right thing ALL the time, whether anyone else sees us or not.

The fact is, God always sees what we do and hears all we say. Any time we have to try to justify our actions, chances are it's an integrity issue.

Things like, *"It's just a little lie"* or *"The Company owes me this." "I deserve more than I have been given so I will just take this item."*

Each and every time we step over the integrity standard, we have stepped further from our morals and values.

There is a simple solution:
  One: Repent for our lack of integrity.
  Two: Refresh your mind with the Word.
  Three: Renew your commitment to integrity.
  Four: Receive the blessings of doing the right things and walking in
      favor with God.

The Right People
· ·

God knows just what we need and when we need it. God also knows who we need and when we need them. God allows all kinds of people to come into our lives for many different reasons. Sadly, Satan also sends people to invade our lives hoping to, in some way, damage us. People teach us lessons we could never know otherwise. All of our emotions are in some way affected by the people we associate with. Those sent by Satan teach us how to lie, steal, kill, cheat, complain, manipulate, gossip, be greedy, selfish, cruel and the list could go on, but you get the point. Thank God, He sends us people to teach us how to love, laugh and live in such a way we become a better person. Almost daily we are influenced by the people around us. Some people will be with you for a lifetime while others are more seasonal and momentary. It is always a good thing to take time to see how the people in your life are influencing you; good and bad. My life has been blessed in so many ways by all the great people God sent my way. And if we are willing to release some of those who infect us, then God has others He will send to bless us and build us up. As the old saying goes, "We are the company we keep."

Placed On Purpose
. . . .

Seek wisdom not relocation! Many times we don't understand why we are in the places we are. Before you lose heart and allow frustration to overtake you, stop for a moment and evaluate your situation. Let's use the workplace as an example. You have a job, maybe not a great one, but, a job none the less. You face many challenges and sometimes difficult people. So you ask, *"Why am I here, Lord?"* There may be several reasons you work where you do.

One, it is possible that some time ago, you asked God to use you in some great way and that is just what He is doing. You may be there because God has given you what you need to help someone there you are around every day. Every person you work with, who does not know Jesus as Lord, needs someone like you to show them.

Two, you may be there just to be a godly example of what a Believer should be and how they should conduct themselves. Jesus was our example in all things. When people want to know what Jesus would do at their work place they should be able to watch you and get that question answered.

Three, sometimes God puts His children in areas just to show His power through them. God said He would bless all we put our hands to do as long as it is right. His anointing on your life can transform the place you work and people will know it was His presence on you that made things happen.

So, shine where you are planted and in time when your work for God is complete, He will promote you to greater things. Just be faithful!

True Friend
· · · · · · · · · · · · · · · ·

Most who consider themselves friends are often just acquaintances. There is a big difference. An acquaintance is someone who knows you and some things about you, but has no investment in you and will separate themselves from you at the first sign of conflict.

A Friend however is someone who knows a lot about you, along with your imperfections and, yet, they still like you and support you. They don't always agree with you, but they are there when others walk away or for a moment distance themselves.

We should all appreciate those acquaintances, but thank God for real friends. I am sure we have all been one or the other at some time. Our goal should be that of being the kind of friend to others that we may one day need for ourselves.

The Best is Yet to Come

It is in times like these we need God the most. There is nothing that would thrill Satan more than for people to allow him to fill their minds with assumptions, imaginations and suggestions.

We do not have a covering from the pains of life but we do have a God who will get us through them. When people are hurting, we don't need all the reasons or answers, we need to pray for the healing that can only come from God's help.

The only winners in life's struggles are those willing to cast every care upon the LORD, Who knows what is best. I have no idea what tomorrow holds, but I, with great expectancy, know WHO holds tomorrow. If God has gone before us as HE promised, then yes, the best is yet to come.

The Cycle
· · · · · · · · · · · ·

God truly has a sense of humor. How many times as a child I would forget something I needed for school; many times really. After all I was a kid with a lot of major stuff on my mind. World-changing stuff you know. Mom would always say it would come back to me one day and I would reap what I had sown, yeah, right. So now I am grown, I think I am, I hope I am, and NOW I am on the way to school to take my daughter something she needed. BUT, I feel her pain. I was young once and had a world of stuff on my mind. Hold on Anna, I'm on the way, and Mom, you were right… again!

Decisions

· · · · · · · · · · · ·

Big results often start with little decisions. You don't just get up one day and run in the big 5 mile race. If you have any hope in completing the race, it is not because you have been practicing for months. It is not because you have the best shoes and gear to run with. It is not because you ran many days when you didn't feel like it. It is not because you even like running. It is simply because you made a DECISION to exercise and running was the avenue you used to do it.

Regardless of what you desire to accomplish in life, it has to start with a heart-felt, life-changing DECISION. So what is it you really would like to do or accomplish? Sit down and ask God to lead you in making those decisions and setting goals to accomplish them. Write them out and put them where you can see them daily.

Then just do it!

Higher
· · · · · · · · ·

Zacchaeus was a man in the Bible who wanted to see JESUS so badly he was willing to climb up in a tree. He hoped to see JESUS as he passed by with the crowd. To his surprise, JESUS stopped and told him to come down because He would be going to his house.

Is there a lesson here for us? Of course!

First, if you are willing to put forth the effort to see JESUS, you can be SURE He will then see you.

Second, the crowd was in JESUS' presence, but Zacchaeus got His attention due to his determination.

Third, always have your house in order because you never know when JESUS might make a special visit.

Lastly, be honest with Jesus and yourself and your life will be fully blessed. Anyone want a better view of JESUS? Then go a little higher.

And all God's children said, AMEN!!!!!!!

Meet The King

· · · · · · · · · · · · · · · · · ·

It was life as usual as the shepherds were watching over their sheep. I'm sure the night was still, the stars shining, and the air cool and refreshing. Who knows the conversation, if any, that was going on when suddenly the Angel appeared with the greatest news ever heard.

The much anticipated Savior had arrived, as was prophesied many centuries before. The stillness of the night was now filled with the glory of the LORD as the Angel spoke. How could one not be fearful of such an encounter with the Host of Heaven? But quickly, excitement drove away the fear. The once quiet spot was now filled with the singing of that Heavenly Choir, *"Glory to God in the highest and on earth peace, good will toward men."*

Sheep or no sheep they could not contain themselves. They had to see HIM; that babe in Bethlehem, the Savior of the World. They walked through the fields God created, breathed the air He provided. Under the drapery of the stars, He placed in the sky above, to get to the place He destined; the stable in Bethlehem. And there they found Him, the Christ child, the King of Kings, the LORD of Lords, the Prince of Peace, Wonderful, Counselor, the Mighty God, Emmanuel, lying in a manger as the Angel had said.

What else was there to do, but WORSHIP!

A Prophecy
· · · · · · · · · · · · · · ·

God has a plan and it is to, in some way, bless you. Even when you think He is not paying any attention to you, He has a plan. He will not allow more than you can handle. He will not allow the enemy to defeat you. God will not allow your situation to overtake you.

He has Angels watching over you. Why? He has a plan! Your hard times will not last much longer. Your redemption is drawing nigh. Shout Amen! Peace is about to overtake you and joy will fill your morning. Why?

Because God has a plan. Hell is trembling and Satan is fearful of this plan. You will be made the head and not the tail. You will be the victor and not the victim. Just hold on a little longer. Your breakthrough is approaching. Your promotion is on God's mind. Square up your shoulders my Beloved, you are about to enter a new level of power and anointing. Well!

Don't fret one bit. Stop the stressing and prepare for the blessing. Well can I get a Witness?

Opportunities
· · · · · · · · · · · · · · · ·

Our days are filled with opportunities to do good. There will always be someone who needs what you have. A smile, a word of encouragement, a helping hand, a prayer, and the list could go on. I really feel our best days are when we have done something good for someone else. Allow the Holy Spirit to show you the needs around you today and do all you can to meet those needs. You will be sowing good seeds that will become a harvest for your time of need.

Reflection

· · · · · · · · · · · · · ·

Lord, You gave me another day.

Now set me to walk Your way.

May everything I say and do,

Be a reflection that honors You.

Prospective

· · · · · · · · · · · · · · · · ·

Today I will look at what I do have and not what I don't have.

I will praise my God and Creator for all He
has done and is doing for me.

I will worship Him for who He is and how He cares for me.

I will not worry over things of which I have no control but
trust my Heavenly Father to work all things for my good.

I choose peace today and refuse frustration and confusion.

I rejoice in the LORD for all I need is in Him.

I will walk in favor and promotion because I am walking with Him.

I will guard my lips and shield my heart from the enemy's attacks.

Today will not be just another day, but the first day of a new beginning.

Let's do this LORD...

Words
· · · · · · · · ·

No matter what you are facing in life, no matter what day, month or year you face it, someone else is still facing more.

Our trials and tests can make us better, or they can make us bitter. Learn from the things you go through and they will be much easier next time around. And remember what we give voice to will most often come to pass. We have creative power in what we say, ssssoooo why not create a great day, starting with praise to God for this day.

Vision

· · · · · · · · ·

LORD, open my eyes today to see beyond the natural things, activities, and events.

By the power of Your Holy Spirit and the Word, let me see into the supernatural.

Let me quickly see the devil and know his tactics and devices working in and on those I may come into contact with.

If I can see, then I can respond with the Word and prayer. Thus, rendering the enemy's attacks useless.

May my desire be, that the power of the supernatural become natural to me, as I follow JESUS in all things.

Amen.

Declaration Of Faith

· ·

LORD, my success today will be determined
by me. Not those around me.

You are with me, therefore if I listen to You, I cannot and will not fail.

You are my strength to stand, to fight and defeat the enemy.

You have given me power, dominion, and authority to
expand my borders and enlarge the tent of my dwelling.

I refuse the lies of the devil, but will gladly heed to Thy Word.

My focus is fixed.

My heart is set.

My spirit is ready.

My mission is clear.

"Take this world for the kingdom of GOD."

OK Jesus, let's roll.

Favor

· · · · · · · ·

LORD, show me favor today! Surprise me with the supernatural.

Encourage me with Your power.

Hold me up in Your strength.

Wrap me up in Your love.

Make mine enemies be still and quiet.

May I truly feel and know Your presence no matter what I face today.

You, LORD, are my God and my hope. I need none other.

Shine

· · · · · · · ·

LORD, until You tell me different, my job is my mission field. Today, I will pass by people who are hurting, lost, confused, and in need of Your love. May my light so shine for You that in some way I can help them know You better.

LORD, let my attitude be encouraging and uplifting. May Your Holy Spirit be upon me so greatly that the enemy has to flee from before me, thus allowing Your love and light to reach those in darkness.

May I be the Church for those who don't attend one, but will have the opportunity to worship with me in some way.

May my time at work also challenge others who know You so that together, we would become an Army for You, LORD.

I pray the only one who regrets meeting me today be the Devil himself.

OK, I'm with you LORD, lead on!

New Day

· · · · · · · · · · · ·

Regardless of my yesterdays, good or bad, I have a brand new day before me.

LORD, before I mess it up in any way, I am giving it to You.

Order my steps, guide my lips, touch my heart, renew my strength, fill my joy and add Your peace.

May the end of this day find me having done all I could to please YOU, in every way.

The Rock
· · · · · · · · · · · ·

The LORD is my rock, and my fortress, and my deliverer, my God, my strength, in Whom I will trust, my shield, and the horn of my salvation, and my high tower." Ps. 18:2

Rock: solid and unmovable.

Fortress: impenetrable place of safety.

Deliverer: one who has the power to completely deliver.

God: Supreme Creator and Being above all beings.

Strength: unstoppable force.

Horn of Salvation: one who is King, able to supply.

High Tower: place of refuge high above the enemy.

Thy Will

· · · · · · · · · ·

LORD, I pray your perfect and complete will be done in my life this week. May I be what you desire, do what you require, love what you admire, learn what you inspire, let go of what you retire, and fan the flames of what you set fire. That should make for a really awesome week.

Lead Me Lord

· · · · · · · · · · · · · · · ·

LORD help me today to walk in your steps. Help me to hear and know Your voice. Help me to seek Your ways and will in all I say and do. Help me to bring honor to Your name. Help me to shine with Your presence so as to push back the darkness of this world. Help me to refuse anything less than what You have desired for me. Help me LORD to be like You. Amen.

Cleansed

· · · · · · · · · · ·

And though our sins be as red as scarlet, He shall make us white as snow. Thank you, LORD, for taking away our sin and cleansing us with the blood of Your only begotten Son, JESUS.

Promise

· · · · · · · · · ·

Thank you God that You, Your Word, Your Son, and Your Holy Spirit are the same yesterday, today and forever.

'CAUSE nothing else is.

Adoration
· · · · · · · · · · · ·

LORD, have I told you lately how much I truly love and adore You.

I can never thank You enough for saving me from a hell I deserved.

I so appreciate every blessing and gift You have given me LORD.

Your favor and mercy have abundantly caused me to prosper. Your presence has filled my life with joy unspeakable and full of glory.

Your Holy Spirit is ever comforting me, teaching me and empowering me for great things.

My life would be worthless if not for You, Father. May the life
You give me bring honor and glory to Your name forever.
Amen and Amen.

Power Of Prayer
· · · · · · · · · · · · · · · · · ·

*"But thou, when thou prayest, enter into thy closet, and when thou
hast shut thy door, pray to the Father which is in secret; and thy
Father which seeth in secret shall reward thee openly." Mt. 6:6*

How many Believers really pray? How many talk with God on a daily
basis? Sadly, for some the tool of prayer is only for cases of extreme need
or emergency. So let's look a little closer at the subject of prayer.

Why is prayer so powerful? It is because genuine prayer consists of 'words'.
Go back with me to the beginning of the planet as we know it. Where
did it all come from? I'm sure you know that God spoke all things into
existence. He did not think it, wish it, or even hope it, but He spoke it.
The words He spoke had the power to create whatever He said. So then,
God gave His highest creation, man, this gift of 'word creation'. This term
means that we have the ability to create our surroundings by the things
we SAY. Note again, words have creative power.

So what do prayers consist of my Beloved? Hopefully, you agree: WORDS.
God invites us to talk with Him through prayer consisting of world
impacting, life changing, devil defeating, and problem solving word power.
That is right!!! Many situations are already being corrected just by the
words we are saying to God as we pray. As our prayers go upward to the
heart of God they move in the earth to meet the needs of men. Therefore
it is critical that our prayers be vocal.

Think about the very term, "silent prayer." There are few things Satan enjoys
more than silent prayer. Prayers, without words actually being spoken.
Some will say, "But brother, God can read our thoughts and knows what
is in our hearts." Yes, I agree that is true. But, He also sees our decision for
salvation in our hearts, but does He not say for us to CONFESS our sins
and to CONFESS Jesus to be our Lord? God's Word also tells us to ASK
when we pray. Why? There is power in our spoken words.

With this being a fact, prayer changes the world around us. Now for prayer to be fully effective, the words we speak MUST line up with God's Word. He cannot and will not honor any word that does not agree with His Word. His Word is total truth and it is eternal. God will always honor His Word. When we pray with words that line up in principle and meaning to His Word, then we can, without doubt, know that our prayer will be answered. God even gave us His Holy Spirit to help us pray so that we can't get it wrong.

It is my desire that we all pray more effectively and sincerely. If you have an active prayer life, I thank God for you. I know that He smiles each time you approach Him through prayer. If we're honest with each other, we would agree that our prayer lives could do with some adjusting by the Holy Spirit. The plans and will of God can be achieved by the prayers of the Saints. Regardless to your current prayer life, seek a greater one with the Lord. It can transform the world around you starting with you.

God's Plan For You
· ·

*"The steps of a good man are ordered by the LORD
and he delighteth in his ways." Ps. 37:23 KJ*

*"The steps of a good man are directed and established by the LORD when
He delights in his way and He busies Himself with His every step." Amplified*

Believe it or not, God has a plan for your life. Say that out loud to yourself, *"God has a plan for my life."* Greater than that, He has a divine plan and a supernatural plan for your life. It is God's desire to bless us in ways our minds cannot even grasp. There is nothing in the Bible that God has done for others that He will not do for us, IF we will do the things they did. John 10:10b Jesus said, *"I am come that they (Believers) might have life (spiritual), and that they might have life more abundantly (supernatural)."*

It is not God's plan that we just live, but that we live in power, authority and dominion. Please Note: the only thing that can block God's plan for our lives is OUR plans. The 'good man' mentioned in the above Scripture is really translated 'God Man.' Jesus said there was only ONE good and that was God. So then, the only way we can be truly good is to be like God. With that being said, who is directing your steps today? Who is the ONE calling all the shots in your everyday life?

Yes, I know we love God, we praise Him, we worship Him and many even faithfully serve Him. BUT, do we trust Him enough to let Him have total control of our lives? Let's be honest, if our lives are a mess right now, spiritually, physically, emotionally, financially or even socially, who is to blame? Who has control? God or Us? Are our finances under His control? Are we following His plans for our health? Does He approve of our relationships? Does the Holy Spirit direct our every step? Are our minds focused on Him and His plans for us?

No matter where we are in life right now, good or bad, God still has a plan. However, we still need a plan and that would be to follow His plans for us. Proverbs 3:6 says, *"In ALL thy ways acknowledge Him, and He shall direct thy paths."* The Amplified Bible says it this way, *"In ALL your ways know, recognize and acknowledge Him, and He will direct and make straight and plain your paths."* There it is, The Plan, "in ALL thy ways!" It is when we seek Him in everything, that His plans are fully known to us. Now we know that God is not going to do everything for us, but will gladly help us succeed if we follow His lead.

Have you ever had to use some type of trouble-shooting to fix something? Like a manual, online assistance, you asked someone who knows or finally just read the instructions. Well the good news is God created the first original trouble-shooting through the Bible, the Holy Spirit, Apostles, Prophets, Teachers, Evangelist, Pastors and mature Believers. While all of these are a great help, most times we would not need them if we simply followed the instruction manual, the Bible.

Jeremiah 29:13 says, *"And ye shall seek me, and find me, when ye shall search for me with all your heart."* The Amplified says, *"Then you will seek Me, inquire for, and require Me (as a vital necessity), and find Me WHEN you search for Me with ALL your heart."* Have you ever misplaced something? Ever notice how you find things you were not looking for that you also needed? Wow, yeah I know! God will sometimes make us search Him out in one area, so He can help us with something we also needed in another area and we didn't even know it at the time. This is a great place for a, Praise the LORD! So if God has a plan then our main plan should be to know it, right? What is the best way to accomplish this? Put it in a journal. Write out a plan for every area of your life; spiritually, physically, financially and also for your relationship, career and even hobbies.

Set both short and long term goals with the help of the Holy Spirit. Don't worry about getting something wrong, He will let you know if it is not in God's plan for you. Once you have your goals written down, gather the information needed to accomplish each goal and start a plan of action to achieve them. If you fail to plan, you plan to fail! Ask God to forgive you for the times you didn't trust Him or follow Him. Allow the Holy Spirit to guide you now and submit to His leading. View your plans often, if not daily. Now, my friend, you are on the way to discovering the Power of God's Plan for your life.

Greater Works

· · · · · · · · · · · · · · · · ·

"Verily, verily, I say unto you, He that believeth on me, the works that I do shall he do also: and greater works than these shall he do; because I go unto my Father." John 14:12

Booker T. Washington said, *"Excellence is to do a common thing in an uncommon way."* How true that is my friends. God created us to do not just ordinary things but extra-ordinary things. Out of God's creation we display His greatest design. He created the Heavens and the Earth but created MAN last; thus saving the best for last. Many people simply exist from day to day but some strive for excellence and abundant life in Christ.

Take just a moment to ask yourself some questions. Where am I currently in my life? What are my goals and what do I want to accomplish? What are my dreams and what am I doing to pursue them? Why do I do the things I do and the way I do them? Is there a better way? Really stop and think on these questions and if you are really serious, write down your response to them.

To keep strife out of your life, do everything with excellence, and be a person of integrity and honesty are three areas we need to focus on for success. It is not the really big things or choices that make us honest and reveal our level of integrity, but it is the everyday things we do. Such as being courteous to others, cleaning up after ourselves, practicing safe and polite driving habits, not breaking in line, putting things back where we got them, tipping for good service and being on time all the time.

Maybe others are not meeting the integrity mark, but you my friend, can and should. Every action has a reaction and every seed brings a harvest; good or bad. It is a bad thing to get to the end of life and have a long list of regrets of not doing the things we could have. But where do I start, one might ask? With doing your BEST at everything you do! Are we currently doing our best in every area of our lives? If not, start now; today. Be the best parent, friend, spouse, neighbor, employee, church member, and the list could go on and on.

Walking in excellence gives satisfaction to your spirit and peace to your mind. There is great joy in accomplishing things with excellence. We break the hold of excuses once we decide on excellence. It starts with a decision and continues with our thought process. When we focus on excellence we operate in excellence and integrity. Philippians 4:8 tells us to think on the things that are true, honest, just, pure, of good report, along with things of virtue and praise.

Winston Churchill said, *"Being responsible is what makes us honorable people. It is the price of greatness."* Regardless of how others are living, or their level of excellence and integrity, it is up to us how we live. Before we can go the extra mile we must decide to go an extra step. It doesn't matter where we start applying excellence and integrity as long as we start. Stop living with regret and start giving everything your absolute BEST. The peace it will bring will make a world of difference.

Remember The Lord

· ·

"But remember the LORD your God, for it is He who gives you the ability to produce wealth, and so confirms His covenant, which He swore to your forefathers, as it is today." Deut. 8:18

The Bible says a lot about remembering. It references remembering over 250 times. We learn very little if we do not have the ability to remember.

It is very important to remember things. Each one of us are who we are today, not just by what we know, but also by what we remember. We would all agree it is pleasant to remember the good things and the good times. But life is not always that easy. We all have some things we would most likely not want to remember, but even those things teach us some type of lesson.

Then there is the danger of focusing so much on the bad that it keeps us from moving forward in life. We should allow our memories to help us grow and mature to become the better person we were created to be. Remembering is as much a part of our daily lives as breathing. If used properly, our ability to remember can bless us in many ways.

While life is full of decisions and choices it is our memory that helps us make many of those decisions and choices. But I must say that of all the things we can and should REMEMBER, God is the most important. Many times the Scriptures tell us to, "Remember the LORD our God." Why? To forget God, is to forget the very One, Who can help us most. It would be easy to take God for granted if we didn't remember all He has done and all that He is to us.

Our God has been, and is still so very good to each one of us. Can I get a big 'AMEN' from someone? Let me be honest by saying when I am feeling sorry for myself, I am not remembering how good God is. When I am fretting over my finances, I am not remembering that He is my supply and provision. When I am overly concerned about my health, I am not remembering that He is my healer. When I am worried about anything, I am not remembering that I should cast my care upon Him, for He cares for me.

God is our Everything. We should daily remember how blessed we are that He loves us so very much. I encourage you to remember and meditate on who God is, what He has done, is doing and has the ability to do for you. Many times the Bible says, *"Remember, least ye forget."* I also encourage you to thank God and praise Him each time you remember His blessings, benefits and favor on your life.

It is a fact that God always remembers us and His promises to us. He is faithful to keep those promises. He is able to protect us and provide for us. Remember, remember and remember again, the goodness of our God and Father. Never forget His benefits or soon they will be gone from us. Ask the Holy Spirit to help you daily, remember the one who not only gave you life, but gave you life more abundantly.

Examine Me Lord

· · · · · · · · · · · · · · · · · · · ·

"Examine me, O LORD, and prove me; test my heart and my mind." Psalms 26:2

Let's be honest! When is the last time you prayed a prayer like this one. Really and seriously prayed for God to take a real close look into our hearts and minds. Not that He does not already know, but are we willing to allow Him to not only look but to reveal what He finds in us.

'Examine' means to inspect someone or something in detail to determine their nature or condition; to investigate thoroughly. Do we really have the nature of God? The Word teaches us that the old man dies and we take on the new man in Christ Jesus. We are called by the Word, "new creatures." That new man should look more and more like Jesus the longer we live in Him. Whereas we once walked in the flesh nature, we now walk in Christ and live by the Spirit of God. What does our nature reveal about who we are in Christ?

'Prove' means to demonstrate the truth or existence of something by evidence or argument. With this in mind, it means to allow God to look at us in line with His Word. His Word is truth! So how close to living the truth are we? There is no doubt whatsoever, that you are living at some level of His truth, but how much is my point. Are we living by what our society says is truth or what God says is truth? Jesus said we could know Him (truth) and that He would make us free. The freedom He offers is nothing less than abundant life in Him.

'Test' means a procedure to establish the quality, performance, or reliability of something. Without a doubt we are valuable to God. Why else would He offer up His only Son for us? But how valuable are we to the Body, where it also counts. If you or I stopped attending Church today, would it even make a difference in that ministry? What impact do we have on others God has put in our path? On a scale of 1 to 10, how reliable are we in the things of God? How well are we performing the task He created us to do?

Asking God to examine, prove, and test us would seem like a tough thing to do. It would be the best thing we could do. We are not asking God to judge us and bring sentence on us, but to simply show us who we are, where we currently are with Him and where He desires us to be. It is God's desire that we become all He has created us to be. When we take a test it reveals what we know and what we don't know. If we seem to fail, in some part, it allows us to know where we need to study more.

David was not seeking God's judgment, but instead David was welcoming God's guidance in the areas he was coming up short. Are you ready to go further, dream bigger, love larger, live more abundantly and spiritually grow stronger? Then pray this Scripture and allow God to reveal some areas that may be hindering your promotion. Don't be afraid of the improvements He is going to make. God is loving and longsuffering toward us so He will not put more on us than we can bear.

God's Provision
· · · · · · · · · · · · · · · · · ·

"The young lions do lack, and suffer hunger: but they that seek the LORD shall not want any good thing." Ps. 34:10

If there is one thing that we can get from this Scripture it is the fact that God will keep His Word and always take care of His Children. But this Scripture says much more than just that. I really like what the Amplified Bible says and reveals: *"The young lions lack food and suffer hunger, but they who <u>seek</u> (inquire of and require) the LORD (by right of their need and on the authority of His Word), none of them shall lack any beneficial thing."*

Please take special note at who is having their needs fully met. Those who <u>seek</u> the LORD. Not everyone is seeking God! There are those who are looking for His hand (supply) but not His face (presence). The Scripture also says, *"We will find God when we search for Him with ALL our hearts."* God will not allow us to have a casual relationship with Him. He wants our whole heart, as well as our undivided attention. Romans 8:28 says, *"And we know that ALL things work together for good to them that love God, to them who are <u>the called</u> according to His purpose."*

Who are "the called?" They are those who have accepted Jesus as their LORD and Savior. Their sins have been washed away by the blood of the Lamb and they are now the Children of God. And with that comes all the blessing of God as well. God is now our Father and He desires to love and help us. But like any good father, He also desires to spend time with us and commune with us. He wants to know we really love Him and desire His presence as well.

Read His Word, receive His promises, but seek His face and ALL you need in every area of your life will be added unto you.

Walk In The Light

· ·

*"For the LORD God is a sun and shield: the LORD will
give grace and glory: no good thing will He withhold
from them that walk uprightly." Psalm 84:11*

This is truly a wonderful Scripture. It reminds us that just as the sun gives light and energy to the Earth, so does God give light and power to His Children. The Bible tells us that we are the children of light and not of darkness. The light of God, His Word and His Holy Spirit allow us to see the truth and know the way of righteousness. Therefore we can walk (live) uprightly and not stumble as those who walk in the dark.

Jesus said He was the, *"Light of the World"* and that He would show us the way to God, and He did. Now that we know Him, we become lights for Him, reflecting His love and mercy to this lost and hurting world. When people see us, they should see Jesus in us. Christians have been entrusted with the responsibility of witnessing the love of Jesus and the grace of God to this world. Many will be lost for eternity if we do not show them the WAY (Jesus).

The above scripture also states that, *God is our shield*. A shield is used for protection during a battle. God is our protection against the attacks of the enemy. He knows how and when we need protection as well. God knows every trick and device of Satan. As long as we stay close to God, we are safe. It is when we refuse His help that we find ourselves in trouble beyond our ability to overcome. Anytime you feel yourself losing spiritual focus, seek the help of the Holy Spirit to get back on track. God will not forsake us in any way as long as we call on Him and trust Him. We are truly covered in His love and grace.

Please note the condition of God's favor on your life, *"no good thing will He withhold from them that walk (live) UPRIGHTLY."* It is God's desire to bless us over and beyond what we can even imagine. It is His will and desire to save, heal, deliver, protect, promote and bless those who follow

His Word and listen to His Holy Spirit. The Bible has given us examples of many others who were blessed abundantly due to their being faithful and living upright before God. We know that God is no respecter of persons and will bless all the same if we obey His Word.

No matter what you may need today, God has the ability to make things happen for you. No good thing means there is NOTHING that is in line with God's Word that He will not give us if we will live and do right before Him. There is much reward in living right before God just as there is much lack in living in disobedience. The Bible reveals to us the ways of righteousness and blessing.

Some things we face are just a test to help us grow and mature spiritually. It is when we are in constant lack that we must examine ourselves and see if we are missing some spiritual truth that may be hindering us in some way. If so, get it right and God will restore the favor and blessings to that area. If all is well, then stay focused and praise Him for His grace and glory.

Dr. Glenn A. Mills

Guiding Word
· · · · · · · · · · · · · · · · ·

"Thy WORD is a lamp unto my feet, and a light unto my path."
Psalm 119:105

As we look around us each day we can hardly believe things have come to the place they are today. The news can be so depressing with all the crime and violence. As the old saying goes, "it's a dog eat dog world" we are living in for sure. We are often hearing of how others are being abused or neglected in some way. Many children seem to be raising themselves because moms and dads are busy with other things. I could go on with a long list of trouble, but there is no need reminding you of something you already see and know. But, I can bring you hope and good news.

God has put before us things that will bring us joy and peace while often challenging us to grow in our faith. I don't know about you but I personally do not like taking tests at all. But when I do take one, there is such joy in knowing that I studied hard and passed the test. There will always be something to test our faith and knowledge. The only way to PASS these many test and trials is to know the answers. I am glad to share with you today that we not only have the answers to life's problem we also have a great Teacher to help us learn the truth.

The BIBLE is our textbook for living and the Holy Spirit is our Teacher. EVERYTHING we will ever need to know is in God's Holy Word. It will give you wisdom, knowledge, understanding, inspiration and revelation. God desires that we receive the joy of passing every test we face. The Holy Spirit is loving, patient and long-suffering with us so that we can learn how to apply God's Word to our lives. Jesus told His followers, *"You shall know the truth and the truth shall make you free."* Free from what, one might ask. Free from sin and shame. Free from guilt of wrong decisions made. Free from our biggest enemy; ourselves. Free from the lies of the Devil. Free to live in the victory and power that God makes available to us.

Our world is suffering because they often refuse the truth of God's Word. Sadly, many Believers don't know the Word much better than those who don't have a relationship with God. Great joy and peace can be found in the precious pages of that Holy Book. Victory and comfort await those who will open their minds and hearts to God's truth. No matter what tomorrow holds the answers are in His Word today.

If a soldier were sent into battle without proper training he would die at the hands of a skilled enemy. But the one who is well trained in the ways of war and defense has what is needed to not only survive, but to conquer and defeat the enemy. It is the same with us. God said, *"My people are destroyed for lack of knowledge."* If we will commit to God's Word and instruction, while being skillfully taught and trained by the His Holy Spirit; we will live in hope and victory.

I trust you will fall madly in love with God's Word. Joy and Peace await you there. Godly wisdom, knowledge and understanding can soon be yours. Make time for the very thing that can give you comfort and direction; The WORD!

Resurrection Power

· ·

Jesus said unto her, "I am the resurrection, and the life; he that believeth in me, though he were dead, yet shall he live." John 11:25

Could you for a moment try to imagine the hearts and minds of those who loved and followed Jesus? They had such great expectations of what they thought He would do and be. Surely they were enjoying the celebration as He rode into Jerusalem the week before His crucifixion. They must have felt honored and privileged to walk there beside Him as the people shouted praises to Jesus. In their relationship with Him you might say they had front row seats.

And then could you again imagine how they must have felt when suddenly Jesus was secretly arrested, wrongfully tried, mercilessly beaten, mockingly paraded through the streets and then cruelly crucified? All were afraid and many were confused and bewildered. How could this have happened? He never hurt anyone or ever did one thing wrong or unlawful. Who would want to take the life of such a good man who just wanted to love and help people? Therein is the reason for the misunderstanding. He was not just a good man doing good things. He, my Beloved, was Jesus Christ, the Son of Almighty God. He did not come just to do good things, He came to die for the sins of the world.

He was much more than good, He was GOD in the flesh! Jesus was not on a vacation to Jerusalem, He was on a destiny for the souls of men. He did not come to stay with men but to obey the Will of the Father. There was no other way for men to be saved but by the blood that had to be given for the remission of sin. As bad a day as it must have been, thank God it was not the end of the story, nor the hopes of mankind. Faithful to His mission, He yielded Himself to the cross and there, He died to finish the work. They placed His body in a borrowed tomb where on the third day He rose with power and great authority. Jesus defeated death, hell and the grave so that we can be saved from our sins and have a relationship with God our Father. Praise God for the work of the cross and the power of the resurrection!

Overcoming By Faith

"For whatsoever is born of God overcometh the world: and this is the victory that overcometh the world, even our faith." I John 5:4

As you may know there are two forces at work in the world we live in today. There are the physical and the spiritual, the seen and the unseen. Because we are physical beings, we tend to mainly live and focus on the things that we can see, hear, smell, taste and touch. But all those things are temporary and are but a dash in our eternity. We live in a physical world, but there is a part of us that is much greater and that is the spiritual nature.

We are most like God not when we operate in the flesh but in the spirit. Jesus took upon Himself a human body to do for us what we could not do for ourselves. He knew the weaknesses and limitations of the physical nature. However, Jesus walked in the Spirit which allowed Him to do the supernatural. After the wilderness temptation, the Word says Jesus returned in great power by the Holy Spirit to begin His ministry of proclaiming God's love, mercy and forgiveness.

Jesus had complete trust that His Father and the Holy Spirit would always lead Him in everything He was to say and do. Everything He did was for the benefit of men and the glory of His Father. What if today that could be said of each one of us? That our one desire was to do the will of our God and Father. What if every day we woke up like Jesus did and spent time with God to first, commune with Him and to second, seek His direction for the day. We could no doubt turn this world upside down for God.

But do we truly believe that this is possible? Faith says it is more than possible; that it can be reality. To fully do the things of God we must have faith in God and His ability to lead, guide and direct us in all things. The more we read God's Word, the more we are strengthened by its truth to believe. The stronger our faith becomes the weaker our doubt becomes.

As we practice our faith, we destroy our doubts. The greater our faith, the more we defeat the enemy and overcome the ways of this world. Allow the Holy Spirit to help you to daily increase your faith so as to please God and overcome this world.

New Assignment
· · · · · · · · · · · · · · · · · · · ·

*"And Moses said I will now turn aside, and see this great
sight, why the bush is not burnt." Exodus 3:3*

I'm sure we have all read the story of Moses and the burning bush in Exodus. There is a lot to be learned from this awesome Scripture. Moses has by one quick decision, put himself far from any dreams he may have had while living in Egypt. Now he is tending sheep for his father-in-law on the backside of the Wilderness. Have you ever been there? Are you there now? A place where you feel alone and often defeated. A place where you just get by. A place where nothing much can be asked or expected of you. The Wilderness! The very name sounds isolating.

But, I have great news. The wilderness isn't a mistake, it is the place of your NEW assignment. We look at the wilderness as the end of our dreams, when in reality it is the place where real dreams begin. If you can survive in the wilderness, you will thrive anywhere else, if you are willing to learn while you are there. The wilderness can teach us things we would not learn anywhere else. If we don't learn and grow, then we will settle for mediocrity, when we could have had the great things that God desires for us.

Let's be honest here, we are all people of great faith, right? Sometimes God has to allow things to happen that will drive us to the wilderness where hopefully we will cry out to Him. When was the last time you really trusted God to do something big in your life or in the life of someone you love? We get busy with our plans and forget He has plans for us. If we keep ignoring Him, we just might find ourselves in the wilderness. WHY? God wants our attention and He will get it, but to our benefit.

Take time today to turn aside from your busy life and look at what God is doing and wants to do. He is not through with you. Your new assignment is waiting for you as soon as He gets your attention.

About The Author

Being a motivational speaker, Glenn Mills fully understands the power of 'words'. He knows words can move us in many ways. They can hurt and they can heal. Words can inspire us to do great things or they can wound us so deeply that we have no desire to do anything. They can challenge us or they can defeat us. Words can make us feel accepted or rejected. People who know how to use words, have the power to change the world for good or evil.

Glenn chooses to use his words for the good of those who read or hear them. It is his desire that his words help people become wiser, feel better about themselves, and challenge them to be all they were created by God to be. It is his hope that his words also bring peace, comfort, joy, laughter, excitement, inspiration, and positive change. It is his prayer that he leave this world a much better place than he found it and that his words do the same.

Glenn hopes you are so inspired by this book that you will share it with others who may need it. His hope is that this book will remain with you for years to come and be a place you can return to when you need the truths written within.

Glenn holds a Doctor of Ministry degree from Covington Theological Seminary in Rossville, Georgia. He currently lives in Temple, Georgia with his wife, Kim. He is the Founder of Open Arms Evangelistic Ministries, Inc. and Glenn Mills Ministries, Inc. He goes wherever God opens the door of opportunity to share His Word, that transforms lives and gives people hope. He can be contacted through www.glennmillsministries.com and glennmillsministries@gmail.com.